WHITE FUNNEL STEAMERS

An advertisement from *In and Around Ilfracombe*, a very informative guidebook published locally during the 1920s and 1930s. The photograph shows the *Cambria* off Ilfracombe in 1922.

WHITE FUNNEL STEAMERS

a photographic legacy

CHRIS COLLARD

The
History
Press

First published 2010

The History Press
The Mill, Brimscombe Port
Stroud, Gloucestershire, GL5 2QG
www.thehistorypress.co.uk

British Library Cataloguing in Publication Data.
A catalogue record for this book is available from the British Library.

ISBN 978 0 7524 5361 3

Typesetting and origination by The History Press
Printed in Great Britain
Manufacturing managed by Jellyfish Print Solutions Ltd

Contents

Introduction and Acknowledgements

The photographs in this book are taken from my own collection, that of my late friend, Mr H.G. (George) Owen, and those friends and correspondents acknowledged below. Its compilation has given me the opportunity to bring to light many photographs which not only have never been published, but which have also rarely been seen.

I am much indebted to the Archivist of the Paddle Steamer Preservation Society, my good friend Andrew Gladwell. In 2007 the society acquired the collection of the late Mr Sydney Clifton Smith Cox, the former managing director of P&A Campbell Ltd. The collection of about 4,000 items consists mainly of sailing bills, posters, publicity material, company documents and correspondence as well as a small number of photographs. Andrew, a fully qualified museum archivist, has very kindly put the collection at my disposal.

The PSPS archives now number about 18,000 items which are stored, catalogued and managed to the highest professional standards in a cellar beneath the ropery in the Chatham Dockyard. Andrew is justifiably proud of his charge and is more than happy to welcome visitors to his 'Aladdin's cave'. I would urge everyone, from the serious enthusiast to those with a passing interest in excursion shipping, to pay him a visit. It is a magical experience!

The White Funnel Fleet of P&A Campbell Ltd was the mainstay of Bristol Channel steamer excursions but the company's long and successful association with the south coast of England was an integral part of its success. This volume covers both areas.

The book has also given me the opportunity to incorporate a certain amount of what might be called 'White Funnel Trivia' – some details of a more domestic nature which have not been included in my six volumes of the company's history but which, nevertheless, form an essential part of its operations.

I wish to express my sincere thanks to all those people who, over the years, have contributed, directly or indirectly, to my researches into paddle steamer history: Dr Donald Anderson, Elaine Bealing, Revd Norman Bird, John Brewer, John Brown, Richard Clammer, Nigel Coombes, Andrew Gladwell, Layton Green, Ken Jenkins, William Lind, John Reypert, Sydney Robinson, Peter Southcombe, Mike Tedstone, Phillip Tolley, Lionel Vaughan and Alan Wakeman.

Also, the late H.A. Allen, Howard Davis, Ernest Dumbleton, Graham Farr, Alfred Harvey, Cyril Hawkins Garrington, John Graham, Jim Hendry, Edwin Keen, Victor Keen, Graham Langmuir, Ernest Nurse, George Owen, Eric Payne, Fred Plant, Dr R.V.C. Richards, Capt. L.G.A. Thomas, Ernest Tucker, Will Widden and Howard Woodberry.

A final word concerning the photographs. Those of known origin are credited accordingly, but in some cases it has been impossible, despite every effort, to establish the exact identity of the photographers. I must express my apologies if any copyright has been inadvertently infringed and hope that this 'omnibus' acknowledgement will serve as an appreciation of all those people in recognition of their work and their invaluable contribution to this book.

I have also included a number of 'snapshot' photographs taken by holidaymakers with 'Box Brownie' type cameras. The quality of their results is somewhat lacking in comparison with the expertise and superior equipment used by the more 'professional' photographers, their interest value outweighs their quality and nevertheless reflects the desire to immortalise happy memories of summer holidays.

Other Titles by Chris Collard

THE HISTORY PRESS

P&A Campbell Steamers – The Victorian Era

P&A Campbell Steamers – The Edwardian Era

On Admiralty Service – P&A Campbell Steamers in the Second World War

White Funnels – The Story of Campbell Steamers 1946–1968

P&A Campbell Pleasure Steamers 1887–1945

P&A Campbell Pleasure Steamers from 1946

Bristol Channel Shipping – The Twilight Years

Bristol Channel Shipping Remembered

A Bristol Channel Album

A White Funnel Album

WHEELHOUSE BOOKS

Special Excursions – The Story of Campbell Steamers 1919–1939

A Dangerous Occupation – A Story of Paddle Minesweepers in the First World War

Before the First World War

The first White Funnel steamer to face the challenge of running excursion steamers in the Bristol Channel was the *Waverley,* owned by the Campbell family of Kilmun and chartered for the 1887 summer season by a syndicate of Bristolians. This simple act led to the establishment of one of the largest and finest fleets of excursion steamers in the United Kingdom. During the early years Peter and Alexander Campbell, having transferred their business from the River Clyde, met with much opposition from local competitors. However, the variety and efficiency of their services, with their expanding fleet of luxuriously appointed vessels, ensured that the White Funnel Fleet eventually eclipsed all of its rivals, and was here to stay!

Waverley arriving at Ilfracombe in the 1890s. *Waverley* became a great favourite with the Bristol public. *The Bristol Channel District Guide* of 1894 stated:

> This popular saloon steamer is equal for speed, reliability and sea-going qualities to any boat of her size afloat, while the care and attention which has yearly been bestowed on her is evinced by her present excellent condition and attractive yacht-like appearance. The luxury and comfort of the Bristol boat render a trip by water very delectable.

With the arrival of a new steamer, the *Ravenswood,* in 1891 the *Waverley* was transferred to the Cardiff to Weston-super-Mare ferry, much to the consternation of the Bristol public. *The Bristol Channel District Guide* continued:

> Deep and widespread has been the regret expressed at the removal of this favourite boat...The Waverley held the premier place in the affections of many nautical Bristolians who from years of practical experience knew how to appreciate her numerous good qualities. It may be of some satisfaction for them to learn, however, that in her new sphere she is equally popular and that she bids fair to reign on that station...(PSPS Archives)

▲ *Ravenswood* in the River Avon in the 1890s. (John York)

◄ *Westward Ho* in the Cumberland Basin lock in 1895. At Bristol passengers normally embarked and disembarked at Hotwells landing stage, a little way downstream from the Cumberland Basin. However, it was sometimes more expedient to use either the basin or sometimes, as on this occasion, the lock itself. (M.J. Ridley)

➤ With her good complement of passengers safely embarked the *Westward Ho* leaves the lock and heads down river. (M.J. Ridley)

➤ *Cambria* outward bound from Bristol on Saturday 8 June 1895, exactly one week after running her maiden trip. She is seen from the Somerset bank a little way upstream from the village of Pill, looking towards the stretch of the river known as Hungroad.

◄ Having set up his large plate camera on its heavy duty tripod the photographer has left it in position to photograph the *Cambria* again, this time on her return journey, sweeping upriver on the ebbing tide after her short cruise to Clevedon.

▼ *Britannia* in the River Avon in the 1890s. She is approaching an inward bound cargo vessel and Capt. Peter Campbell can be seen at the telegraph on the port bridge wing. He is, no doubt, slowing her down in order to pass the oncoming ship safely. Such manoeuvres were often 'tight squeezes' in the narrow confines of the River Avon. (M.J. Ridley)

▲ *Britannia* in the River Usk in the 1890s.

▲➤ *Ravenswood* leaving Newport in the 1890s. (Layton Green Collection)

➤ *Cambria* and the sailing vessel *Rhone* in the Cumberland Basin in the 1890s.

▲ Birnbeck Pier, Weston-super-Mare, with the *Ravenswood* alongside the north jetty. The photograph was probably taken during the late 1890s but certainly before 1902 when a new lifeboat house was under construction on the south side of the bridge, which connected the island to the mainland, in order to house a new larger lifeboat, the *Colonel Stock*, from May 1903. This replaced the original lifeboat house of 1889 which is visible on the right of the bridge. The low water pier under construction can be seen on the left. (PSPS Archives)

▲ Birnbeck Pier low water jetty under construction. The building of the low water pier began in the early 1890s and was intended to enable the steamers to berth at any state of the tide. It was initially completed in 1898 but its close proximity to the rocks, coupled with the strong tidal currents which swirled around the island, made landings difficult and potentially dangerous. It was severely damaged on 11 September 1903 in a ferocious storm which also demolished much of the wooden north jetty. The latter was quickly replaced with a steel structure but re-construction of the low water pier proved to be an extensive undertaking.

In addition the building of extra facilities on Birnbeck Island, including a water chute and ice rink, impeded passenger access and delayed its official opening until Whitsun of 1909. However, the pier remained most unpopular with the ships' masters and was rarely used. It was eventually demolished during the winter of 1921/1922.

The photograph shows, on the right, the construction of the platform between the pier and the lifeboat house which was to support the ice rink and was probably taken during 1907 or 1908. It is unusual as it shows a steamer berthed at the pier. The steamer is the *Waverley* and as the jetty was not operational at that time she was probably making an experimental call. (PSPS Archives)

▲ *Bonnie Doon* in the Avon in the early 1900s. The *Bonnie Doon* was a useful little vessel, equally suited to running both long day trips to Ilfracombe and beyond and short trips in the upper reaches of the channel, as well as serving the company on the south coast. She was already twenty-three years old when she joined the White Funnel Fleet in 1899 and, despite being fitted with a more 'modern' larger diameter funnel in 1907, retained her somewhat antiquated appearance to the end of her career. (Pincock Brothers, Bristol)

▲➤ *Bonnie Doon* off Penarth, 1910/1912. She was laid up at the end of the 1912 season, and with the advent of the new vessels *Lady Ismay* in 1911 and *Glen Avon* in 1912 she was found to be surplus to requirements. She was advertised for sale and eventually sold to Dutch ship-breakers in October 1913. (John York)

➤ *Albion* arriving at Ilfracombe in 1899. The *Albion,* like the *Bonnie Doon,* was a very versatile steamer, dating from 1893, which joined the White Funnel Fleet in 1899 to run in the Bristol Channel and on the south coast. Shortly before the First World War the company were considering lengthening her and plating in her bow, bringing it up to the level of her promenade deck thus extending her forward saloon. However, her requisitioning by the Admiralty for service as a minesweeper in 1915 caused the postponement of that plan. (PSPS Archives)

▲ *Albion* in the Avon in the 1900s. On 2 September 1917 the *Albion,* while on Admiralty service as HMS *Albyn,* sustained a direct hit to her stern during a bombing raid at Dunkirk. Repairs were effected which allowed her to continue with her war service, but on her return to Bristol in February 1919 a survey revealed that the after part of the ship had been twisted by the fire caused by the bomb. The ship herself was beyond economic repair and she was broken up at Troon but her engines, still in perfectly good condition, were removed for installation in the company's new steamer, *Glen Gower,* then under construction at the nearby Ailsa Shipbuilding Co. yard. (PSPS Archives)

➤ *Glen Rosa* in the Merchant's dock, Bristol, in the early 1900s. The third in this trio of lesser-known Campbell steamers, the *Glen Rosa* joined P&A Campbell Ltd in 1898, after having been purchased and operated by Capt. Alec Campbell on his own account during the previous year. Although once again a rather antiquated looking vessel, dating from 1877, she proved herself to be a much valued member of the fleet in both the Bristol and English Channels.

▲ *Glen Rosa* in the Cumberland Basin in the spring of 1911. During the previous winter she had been fitted with a port-holed after saloon. At the same time the large windows of her forward saloon were correspondingly altered. She too was requisitioned by the Admiralty, and from 1917 became part of the 'Swansea Paddlers', keeping the Bristol Channel approaches clear of mines. At the end of the hostilities she was found to be beyond economic repair and was broken up at Bristol in 1920. (John York)

▲➤ *Ravenswood* leaving Cardiff in the 1900s. She is leaving at about half tide, when the dredged channel to and from the East and West Bute Dock entrances, (known as 'the drain'), was surrounded by mud flats. Steamers and sailing vessels can be seen resting on the mud waiting to enter the docks. (PSPS Archives)

➤ Long before the building of the Portway, the riverside road between Avonmouth and Bristol, the *Britannia* makes her way down the Avon Gorge in the 1900s.

▲ *Waverley* at Bristol in the 1900s.

▲ *Britannia* at anchor off Clovelly in the 1900s.

▼ *Cambria* at anchor off Newquay, 1906/1907. During the years before the First World War occasional trips were run to the north Cornish resort, via Ilfracombe, from either Bristol or Cardiff. The distance involved made for a long day out with a departure time of about 6.00a.m. and a return time of midnight, or even the early hours of the following day. (PSPS Archives)

Cambria disembarking passengers at Ilfracombe in 1908.

Ravenswood heads out of Ilfracombe into a choppy sea during 1909. (PSPS Archives)

Cambria (above) and *Britannia* (below) leaving Ilfracombe during the wet and windy summer of 1910. (PSPS Archives)

◄ *Cambria* arriving at Ilfracombe c.1909/1911. Ilfracombe pier was a hive of activity, often likened to a busy railway station. At the height of the seasons, with as many as six or more steamers arriving and departing several times per day, the number of passengers who passed through the pier gates was considerable. The notebooks which recorded that information were stored in a shed on the pier. During a severe winter gale (it is believed sometime during the First World War), a part of the roof was torn off and the record books became saturated by the rain. Unfortunately the 'soggy' pulp was beyond recovery and was destroyed! (PSPS Archives)

▲ Proudly wearing his 'Signalman' cap is Samuel Morman, a long-standing employee of Ilfracombe Pier in the pre-First World War years. With so many steamers coming and going his job was of the utmost importance. He was responsible for hoisting the flags which indicated which steamer was to berth next, and at which berth. Any mistake on his part could have had serious consequences!

Ilfracombe harbour employees on the pier around 1910. (PSPS Archives)

▼ *Westward Ho* leaving Ilfracombe on 1 September 1911. The 'Hospital Trip' referred to in the photographer's caption was the annual charity trip run by the company, the proceeds of which were donated to a local hospital. The *Westward Ho* has just backed away from the stone bench and is about to be canted around on her stern rope in readiness to steam stern first into the open water before turning up channel. (PSPS Archives)

▲ The Ilfracombe Pier rope handlers, with Pier Master Fred Birmingham, on 22 May 1913. Like the job of the signalman, rope handling was also a highly skilled job. Fred Birmingham and his team gained a reputation for speed and efficiency not only by ensuring that the steamers were rapidly 'turned around' in order to maintain their demanding schedules, but also that the passengers were embarked and disembarked safely, quickly and courteously.

▼ *Westward Ho* at the stone bench, Ilfracombe, in 1912.

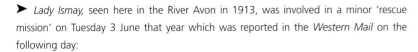

▲ *Cambria* leaving Ilfracombe c.1909/1911. (PSPS Archives)

▲ *Lady Ismay* at Bristol in the spring of 1913. Astern of her, in the distance, is the paddle steamer *Brighton,* owned by Pockett's Bristol Channel Steam Packet Co. Ltd of Swansea, and opposite, at the Mardyke Wharf, the *Britannia. Lady Ismay,* which entered service in July 1911, was the first of four paddle steamers built for the company by the Ailsa Shipbuilding Co. of Troon. All of them were fine ships, built more for economy of running rather than speed. Photographs of the three subsequent vessels are to be found in later chapters but the *Lady Ismay*'s short life ended when she fell victim to an enemy mine in December 1915 while on Admiralty service.

➤ *Lady Ismay,* seen here in the River Avon in 1913, was involved in a minor 'rescue mission' on Tuesday 3 June that year which was reported in the *Western Mail* on the following day:

> There was some excitement among the passengers on the steamer *Lady Ismay* yesterday evening when she was returning to Bristol from a cruise to Clevedon. She was signalled by the liner *Royal Edward* and for a time the passengers were left wondering what was the purpose as both vessels were slowing down. Five passengers who had gone aboard the liner to see friends off for Canada failed to respond to the 'All ashore' bell, and the *Royal Edward* had steamed from Avonmouth with them. They were quickly transferred to the *Lady Ismay*, thankful that they had not been taken on an involuntary trip to Canada.

The *Royal Edward* and her sister ship, *Royal George,* of Canadian Northern Steamships Ltd, began their service between Avonmouth and Canada in the spring of 1910. Both were a little over 11,000-tons gross and ran to Montreal in summer and Halifax in winter. It was common practice for the White Funnel steamers to escort the ships between Avonmouth and Clevedon on both their arrivals and departures.

▲ Passengers aboard the *Cambria* at Ilfracombe on 16 June 1913.

▲ A noon departure from Cardiff for the *Waverley* in 1912/13. On the left, standing between the entrances to the East and West Bute Docks, is the terracotta brick building of the former Bute Docks & Railway Co., dating from 1865. Despite the many changes to this area of the city this magnificent landmark remains in its prominent position overlooking what is now Cardiff Bay.

◄ *Waverley* outward bound in the Avon in 1914. The *Waverley*'s appearance changed in 1911 when her bridge was moved forward of the funnel and portholes replaced her large saloon windows, except those at the after end of the saloon. She ran on the south coast for that season but returned to Bristol Channel service in the following year. In fact she maintained the Cardiff to Weston ferry until 1916.

The late Ernest Dumbleton, who worked in her dining saloon during those years, told of an incident towards the end of the 1916 season. It was a very rough evening at Weston and although the ropes were put ashore at the pier it was impossible for her to make fast. She was hit by a very heavy sea which smashed the after end of the saloon. The sea poured into the ship and took with it the door, complete with the bosun floating on it! On arrival at Cardiff a 'human-chain' of buckets was formed in order to clear the saloon of water. This was her last sailing before being requisitioned by the Admiralty in May 1917. Together with the *Glen Rosa,* the *Waverley* was broken up at Bristol in 1920.

Between the Wars

At the end of the First World War the Campbell fleet had diminished from thirteen to eight vessels: *Ravenswood, Glen Avon, Cambria* and *Glen Usk,* which re-entered service between June and September 1919, and *Britannia, Barry, Westward Ho* and *Devonia* which commenced sailing between April and July 1920.

All of the pre-war competition had disappeared but new adversaries arrived by way of Tucker's Yellow Funnel Fleet of two paddle steamers, *Lady Moyra* and *Lady Evelyn,* and the screw steamer *Robina.* Although intense rivalry ensued, the 'Yellow Funnels' made little headway against the 'White' and they vanished from the scene at the end of the 1921 season, the two paddle steamers re-appearing as part of the Campbell fleet in 1923. The *Albion*'s engines also re-appeared in the new steamer, *Glen Gower,* in 1922. In the Bristol Channel the White Funnel Fleet now reigned supreme.

▲ Lynmouth in 1920. Offshore, the Yellow Funnel steamer, *Lady Moyra*, is disembarking her passengers while the *Britannia* arrives to disembark hers.

◄ *Ravenswood* in the Merchant's dock, Bristol, having just been fitted with a new foremast, March 1921. (Edwin Keen)

▲ *Britannia* leaving Ilfracombe in 1922. Her firemen are piling on the coal for a speedy crossing to Clovelly.

◄ *Britannia* (left) and *Cambria* at anchor off Ilfracombe in 1922.

◄ *Ravenswood* leaving Ilfracombe in the 1920s. She appears to be flying her flags at half mast but this is not necessarily the case. The flags were usually hoisted prior to the vessels' arrivals at their ports of call and were lowered again on leaving. The thrifty Campbell brothers recommended this course of action to avoid their excessive wear, tear and frequent replacement.

▼ *Lady Moyra* arriving at Ilfracombe in 1923.

Britannia arriving at Ilfracombe on Easter Monday 1923.

◄ *Glen Gower* and *Lady Moyra* at Ilfracombe on Thursday 14 August 1924. (H.G. Owen) The stern of the *Cambria* can be seen on the right. Mr Owen notes on the back of the photograph, 'A very wet day. *Cambria* was due to go to Bideford but was cancelled owing to heavy rain'.

▼ *Westward Ho* arriving at Ilfracombe on Monday 31 August 1925.

▲ *Glen Gower* leaving Swansea in 1925.

◀ *Ravenswood* in the Avon in the 1920s.

➤ *Cambria* ashore on Rillage Point, Ilfracombe, on Wednesday 12 July 1926. Her grounding had been caused by thick fog and was attended by the Ilfracombe lifeboat, *Richard Crawley,* which can be seen alongside her port quarter. Of her 146 passengers, 50 were taken to Ilfracombe by the lifeboat, some were taken by the local boatmen and some went by road.

The *Glen Usk* can be seen standing by offshore. The *Cambria* refloated on the afternoon tide and made her way to the pier where temporary repairs were made, although there was little damage. As a precaution she entered Hill's dry dock at Bristol on the following day for a survey and permanent repairs before re-entering service on 22 July. (PSPS Archives)

Lady Moyra arriving at Mumbles in 1927. (H.G. Owen)

▲ *Glen Gower* and *Lady Moyra* at the stone bench, Ilfracombe, on Saturday 3 September 1927. (H.G. Owen)

➤ *Britannia* embarking passengers off Lynmouth in the 1920s.

▼ *Lady Moyra* backs out of Ilfracombe having been berthed between *Cambria* and *Glen Gower* at the stone bench, August 1928. (H.G. Owen)

▲ *Glen Avon* arriving at Weston in the 1920s.

◄ *Glen Usk* leaving Ilfracombe in 1929.
(H.G. Owen)

▲ *Cambria* in the Avon in the 1920s.

➤ With Capt. Oswald Morris striding across the bridge the *Britannia* arrives at Ilfracombe on an Easter sailing in 1929. Note that the forward saloon portholes have not yet been lined – a job to be undertaken during the Easter to Whitsun 'lay up'period when only the Cardiff to Weston ferry steamer – (usually the *Glen Avon*) – would be in service. (H.G. Owen)

◄ *Glen Avon* at Birnbeck pier, Weston-super-Mare, on Tuesday 14 May 1929. There is more to this unremarkable photograph of the *Glen Avon* than appears at first sight. A note in the company's memorandum book for the above date states, 'Prime Minister Stanley Baldwin travelled from Weston to Cardiff on the 7.05p.m. sailing'. This photograph was taken on that occasion. Mr Baldwin, with his wife at his side, can be seen in front of the bridge, both of them waving to the crowd on the pier. The Conservative Party leader was on the campaign trail for the forthcoming general election and had arrived in Weston late that afternoon from Plymouth.

The newspapers reported that between 4-5,000 people were present on Birnbeck Island to greet him. The *Glen Avon* arrived at the pier at about 6.30p.m. having spent a few uncomfortable hours, in very blustery conditions, at anchor offshore over the low water period. After the steamer's departure the Prime Minister and his wife retired to the chartroom, which had been placed at their disposal, but Mr Baldwin very soon joined Capt. Bernard Hawken on the bridge. A call was made at Penarth, where a large crowd of supporters had assembled, and then on to Cardiff where the pier head was thronged with people including the official welcoming party of the city's dignitaries.

Mr and Mrs Baldwin stayed overnight as guests of the Earl of Plymouth at St Fagans Castle, just outside the city. On the following afternoon Mr Baldwin addressed an open-air meeting at Tredegar House, Newport, and in the evening a mass meeting at Cardiff's Empire Theatre. Mr Baldwin's endeavours, however, were in vain. The election, which took place on 30 May 1929, was won by Mr Ramsay McDonald's Labour Party. (PSPS Archives)

► ▲ *Glen Avon* leaving Weston on the above occasion. It was an overcast day with a strong westerly wind and the *Glen Avon* was the only vessel to complete all her scheduled sailings – four round trips between Cardiff and Weston. The *Glen Usk* ventured no further than Cardiff on her day trip from Bristol to Ilfracombe, and the *Ravenswood*'s day trip from Newport to Weston and Barry was cancelled.

► Ilfracombe Pier in the early evening of Sunday 30 June 1929. Mr Owen notes, 'Left to right - *Lady Moyra* from Swansea and Mumbles. *Glen Usk* from Port Talbot. *Glen Gower* from Bristol, Clevedon, Cardiff, Barry and Lynmouth. *Britannia* and *Cambria* have already sailed. Rained all day until 4p.m.' (H.G. Owen)

◄ *Glen Gower* at Ilfracombe on Easter Monday 21 April 1930. (H.G. Owen)

▼ *Westward Ho* arriving at Weston in 1929. (H.G. Owen) She is without passengers, after lying at anchor offshore over the low water period when berthing at the pier was not possible.

➤ A unique photograph of the *Lady Moyra* arriving at Padstow in 1931 or 1932. The occasional visits to Padstow of the 1930s replaced those of the pre-war years to Newquay, owing to the fact that the slightly shorter journey down the Cornish coast enabled the steamers to make cruises out of Padstow. Those cruises attracted large numbers of passengers and gave a very welcome boost to the day's takings. The *Lady Moyra* was the steamer which made the first post-war visit to Padstow on Sunday 12 July 1931. (John Brewer Collection)

▼ *Glen Usk* leaving Bristol on 21 May 1933. (Edwin Keen)

▲ *Glen Gower* arriving at Ilfracombe on Wednesday 9 August 1933. (H.G. Owen)

➤▲ *Britannia* arriving at Ilfracombe in 1933. (H.G. Owen)

▼ A handful of passengers board the *Westward Ho* at Dartmouth on a wet day in either 1932 or 1933. During those seasons she was based, as an experiment, at Plymouth and ran trips to a variety of ports and resorts, eastward as far as Bournemouth and westward as far as Penzance. Even in the exceptionally fine summer of 1933 passenger figures were poor and the experiment was not repeated. (Richard Havard Collection)

▲ An off service day for the *Westward Ho* at the Pier Head, Cardiff, in 1935. (H.G. Owen)

▼ *Glen Usk* arriving at Swansea in 1935. (H.G. Owen)

▼➤ *Ravenswood* at the Harbour Commissioners' Landing Stage, Newport, in 1936.

◄ *Glen Avon* leaving Cardiff c.1938/1939. Taken from *Westward Ho* with Capt. Horace Rumsam on the bridge. (Edwin Keen)

▼ *Britannia* in the Avon on Whit Monday 29 May 1939

A Difficult Day

The excursion steamer business was, and still is, like all outdoor seasonal ventures, predominantly dependent on the unpredictable British weather. The steamer operators prayed for long spells of warm sunshine and calm seas to put 'feet on decks' in order to generate sufficient revenue in half a year to cover their expenditure for a whole year, and to make an honest profit into the bargain.

Furthermore, they had to ensure that their timetables were so carefully planned that all of their steamers were used to their full capacity and lost no opportunity to pick up passengers at as many landing places as possible – the Campbell brothers were experts at that! Over the years the intricacies of traffic management had been honed to perfection; an extraordinary feat considering the added burden of the high rise and fall of the Bristol Channel tides. However, things did occasionally go wrong, and when they did they went wrong in spectacular style!

This chapter illustrates the complexities of dealing with unforeseen problems which involved last-minute decisions being made between the traffic manager in Bristol; the Weston, Cardiff, Barry, Minehead, Lynmouth and Ilfracombe agents, as well as the masters of five steamers and also the Minehead boatmen. Tuesday 13 August 1935 was, indeed, a difficult day!

The first two weeks in August were, traditionally, the peak of the company's busiest time of the year, when every steamer was needed in order to cope with the anticipated heavy traffic. Unfortunately, on Tuesday 13 August 1935 the Bristol Channel was three steamers 'down'. The *Cambria* was laid up in Bristol for the whole of the season undergoing major repairs and maintenance to her engines and paddle wheels, refurbishment of her saloons, the construction of an after deckhouse and the fitting of a new funnel. The *Ravenswood* was alongside her at the Underfall Yard undergoing paddle wheel repairs and the *Britannia* was off service at Cardiff. This meant that the *Westward Ho* and *Glen Avon* were scheduled to maintain the Cardiff to Weston ferry as best they could, while the *Waverley, Glen Usk* and *Devonia* took their scheduled down-channel trips which were:

Dept. Time	Steamer	Route
09.15	**Waverley** (Capt. Bernard Hawken)	Avonmouth for Clevedon, Barry, Lynmouth and Ilfracombe.
16.40		Ilfracombe for Lynmouth, Barry, Weston, Clevedon and Avonmouth.
08.30	**Glen Usk** (Capt. Edward Calvert)	Barry for Minehead, Lynmouth, Ilfracombe, Clovelly and Lundy. (A connecting train left Riverside station, Cardiff, for Barry Pier, at 07.32).
16.30		Lundy for Clovelly, Ilfracombe, Lynmouth, Minehead and Barry Pier and train to Cardiff.
08.45	**Devonia** (Capt. William Riddell)	Swansea for Mumbles, Ilfracombe.
10.40		Ilfracombe for a cruise to Lynmouth and return to Ilfracombe. (The 10.40 sailing to Lynmouth was also advertised as a Day Trip returning from Lynmouth at 16.15 after her cruise to Porlock Bay)
14.30		Ilfracombe on cruise to Porlock Bay with call at Lynmouth on return.
17.15		Ilfracombe for Mumbles and Swansea.
19.20		Swansea for 2 hour cruise around *Scarweather* light vessel.

The *Waverley* arrived at Ilfracombe at 14.11. She was then due to remain at the pier until her return sailing. The *Glen Usk* arrived at Ilfracombe and set off at 11.45 with a good complement of passengers for Clovelly and Lundy, and the *Devonia* arrived at Ilfracombe on time to perform her 10.40 sailing to Lynmouth.

There was, however, a problem up channel. Owing to their schedules it was impossible for either the *Glen Avon* or the *Westward Ho* to take the 15.00 afternoon trip from Weston to Barry. It was decided, therefore, that the *Devonia,* after landing her day return passengers at Lynmouth at 11.30, would proceed light – (i.e. without passengers) – to Weston in order to perform the 15.00 crossing. Consequently, at Ilfracombe the passengers who intended taking the *Devonia*'s morning cruise to Lynmouth were informed that this would not now be possible as the steamer would not be returning; she would land only day trip passengers.

The *Devonia* duly made her way up channel. The 247 passengers which she embarked at Weston and deposited at Barry were to return to Weston in the *Westward Ho*, which was detailed to make a detour to pick them up on her 17.15 sailing from Cardiff.

After her call at Barry the *Devonia* returned to Ilfracombe, again without passengers. Her scheduled afternoon cruise to Porlock Bay, with a call at Lynmouth on the return to embark her day trip passengers which she had landed in the morning, was taken by the *Waverley.* As a consequence of this substitution the *Waverley* was 45 minutes late leaving on her return journey to Avonmouth.

The *Devonia* arrived at Ilfracombe, embarked her Mumbles and Swansea passengers and departed at 18.45, an hour and a half late. She arrived at Swansea at 20.45 to find that the queue of nearly 650 passengers who intended taking her evening trip had long since gone home, so her cruise around the *Scarweather* light vessel was cancelled!

The traffic manager, with hindsight, probably regretted his decision to send the *Devonia* from Lynmouth to Weston and then from Barry to Ilfracombe light, simply to take a fifty-minute crossing from Weston to Barry. The total fares of the 247 passengers on that trip would barely have covered her afternoon's coal bill – if at all! Far better to have cancelled the Weston to Barry crossing than to have missed the two-hour evening cruise with 650 passengers.

Meanwhile, the *Glen Usk* had encountered problems. On her outward journey she had been slightly delayed by embarking her passengers from the boats at Lynmouth. Consequently she left Ilfracombe fifteen minutes late and arrived off Clovelly at 13.10. The boats used to land and embark passengers at Clovelly were smaller than those at Lynmouth and Lundy. Furthermore, they had to land the passengers on the pebble beach by way of a somewhat rickety plank. This operation could be a slow process even under the calmest of conditions, but on this day it was made even more difficult by the fickle fresh wind which veered and backed between the north-east and north-west and sent a nasty surf up the beach.

However, with the transfer of passengers safely accomplished she set off for Lundy at 13.40, now forty minutes behind schedule.

On arriving at the island the large number of passengers who wished to land were taken ashore but once again the wind made progress slow. In fact, by the time all of the passengers had been landed it was time to start embarking them again. She left Lundy an hour late at 17.30 for *Clovelly* where she anchored off shore at 18.32. This time landing and embarking took even longer and it was not until 19.21 that she was under way again, an hour and fifty minutes late.

On her arrival at Ilfracombe at 21.02 Capt. Calvert was informed by the agent, Fred Birmingham, that to avoid further delay her Lynmouth call had been cancelled. The Lynmouth-bound passengers had been sent home by bus, and those who were to board her at Lynmouth, to return to Minehead and Barry, were being taken to Minehead by bus. Therefore Capt. Calvert left Ilfracombe at 21.20 and proceeded straight to Minehead. The fact that on her arrival at Minehead the tide would be too low for her to berth at the pier had, of course, been realised. Mr Birmingham had arranged for eight Minehead boatmen to await her arrival off shore, four in motor boats and four in shallow draft punts.

As soon as the *Glen Usk* anchored off Minehead pier at 23.15, the four motor boats embarked the passengers and began to make their way to the shore. At Minehead the beach shelves very gradually and when the boats were as far in as their drafts allowed they were still surrounded by about a foot of water. The punts then came alongside them, transferred their passengers and they, in turn, headed for the shore. When they had reached their limit, in about six inches of water, the boatmen donned their waders, stepped over the side and carried every passenger ashore, all 160 of them!

Having completed the disembarkation the boatmen then set about embarking the 36 passengers bound for Barry. The whole operation was completed without a hitch. The *Glen Usk* weighed anchor at 23.48 and arrived at Barry at 00.51, nearly three and a half hours late, where a special train awaited the Cardiff passengers.

As for the ship's crew, with all its frustrations, it was all in a day's work, urbanely summed up by Capt. Calvert's entry in the log book:

Fresh NNE to NNW wind with a nasty sea on beaches at Lynmouth, Clovelly and Lundy Island, otherwise a fine day.

Surely a masterpiece of understatement!

Glen Usk arriving at Ilfracombe. (H.G. Owen)

▲ *Waverley* arriving at Ilfracombe. (H.G. Owen)

◄ *Devonia* leaving Ilfracombe. (H.G. Owen)

FOUR

The South Coast

Before the First World War

In June 1897 a Naval Review was held in Spithead to celebrate Queen Victoria's Diamond Jubilee. The Campbell brothers sent their elite trio, *Westward Ho, Cambria* and *Britannia,* south for the occasion. So successful was their visit that they sent the *Cambria* back to Hampshire for August and September. This marked the beginning of a long association with the south coast. From 1898 to 1902 the *Cambria* was the principal steamer, supported by either the *Glen Rosa* or *Albion.* Running mainly from Southampton, Portsmouth and Bournemouth the sailings extended from Swanage to Brighton, including the Isle of Wight, with regular trips to Cherbourg and occasional visits to Boulogne.

Despite intense competition the Hampshire-based sailings were reasonably successful, but an even more lucrative proposition presented itself towards the end of 1901. The Brighton, Worthing & South Coast Steamboat Co. found itself in serious financial difficulties and their superb paddle steamer *Brighton Queen,* built in 1897 by the Clydebank Shipbuilding & Engineering Co. Ltd, was offered for sale. The Sussex coast was another area ripe for development so the Campbell brothers bought her on their own account. She was altered 'Campbell-fashion' at considerable expense and began running from Brighton in 1902. At the end of that season the company abandoned its Southampton base and transferred its south coast headquarters to Brighton from 1903, the brothers having sold the *Brighton Queen* to the limited company in May of that year.

Some time in the 1900s a booklet appeared, written by Reginald Arkell, entitled *Marine Excursions by the South Coast Steamers of P&A Campbell Ltd*. It was a delightful booklet which gave a brief, informative guide to the resorts visited by the White Funnel steamers, written in the somewhat quaint but eloquent style of the period. The first paragraph of Mr Arkell's introduction states:

> It is ten o' clock of a glorious summer morning, and, seen from the pier, Brighton's magnificent seafront is bathed in golden sunshine. The soft breeze that comes up from the south tempers the increasing warmth of a cloudless sky, but it is not sufficient in strength to trouble the face of the waters. The sea is as smooth as glass, and there is scarcely a ripple on the shore. Along the deck of the pier the tide of humanity sets in one direction. No one thinks of remaining on land on such a day. All are bound for the landing stage where one or other of Messrs. P&A Campbell's fine pleasure steamers lies at its moorings. Down the gentle incline of the gangway there is a constant stream of merry voyagers. All have caught the happy spirit of this glorious hour, and everyone is impatient to be gone. Courteous hands busy themselves attending to the needs of passengers. The signal is given for the moorings to be released and, imperceptibly almost, the beautiful vessel glides out into the horizon.

Albion arriving at Eastbourne, 1913/1914. During her spell in Hampshire an unusual event was reported in a Bournemouth newspaper in 1900:

The passenger liner *Briton*, bound from Cape Town to Southampton, was unfortunately disabled when almost home, and had to anchor in the channel about nine miles off Bournemouth on the evening of Thursday 26 July. It so happened that the Bournemouth excursion steamer *Albion*, on a twilight cruise with a large number of passengers, communicated with the well-known liner, the passengers on which were eager to obtain the latest news from home and from South Africa. (The Boer War had started in October 1899). All newspapers on board the *Albion* were speedily transferred, the ladies readily proffering their handkerchiefs that the journals might be the more readily thrown on board...The Dukes of Norfolk and Marlborough and Lady Sarah Wilson were prominent amongst those who sought news from the *Albion*'s passengers. The well-known Bohemian Concert Party, who happened to be on board the *Albion*, were foremost in the musical celebration of the occasion. The *Briton*'s band was mustered on the top deck and played a number of patriotic airs, the choruses being vocally rendered by the crews and passengers of both vessels. The six hundred passengers on the excursion steamer returned to Bournemouth highly delighted at the interesting and unexpected experience, after giving hearty cheers for Captain Henry Chidgey and his crew for the consideration shown in taking advantage of the occasion.

Brighton Queen arriving at Eastbourne in the 1900s. My copy of Mr Arkell's guide book, which dates from about 1911, continues with a laudatory article on the *Brighton Queen*, and states:

This magnificent pleasure steamer, which is so popular a visitor to the south coast during the summer months, is one of the finest boats in the famous "White Funnel Fleet" of Messrs. P&A Campbell Ltd. of Bristol. During her long connection with Brighton she has so completely passed into the picture and won so many friends that it is difficult to imagine what the Queen of Watering Places would be without her. Certainly Brighton possesses no attraction that can compare with the 'Queen's Queen', as she has been aptly styled, and at every town along the coast at which she calls the same thing can be said. Visitors and residents alike have a feeling bordering on affection for the beautiful vessel, while at Boulogne her arrival is more eagerly looked for than that of any other boat paying periodical visits from the English coast...

One hundred persons can be accommodated at a time in the handsomely appointed dining and tea rooms, and a comfortable lounge and bar will also be found on the lower deck...

A special tribute is due to the officers, agents and others who ensure the comfort and safety of passengers. The majority have been long in the service of the company and are consequently able to anticipate the wishes of those on board before any request has been preferred. They constitute a happy family, and not being divided against itself, the House flourishes.

Vive La Reine

Captain John West, master of the Brighton Queen from 1902 to 1913. Capt. West died suddenly on 3 April 1914. His obituary in the *Western Mail* stated:

The death occurred, with painful suddenness, at his residence in Hotwells, Bristol, on Thursday afternoon, of Captain John West, the Commodore of the White Funnel Fleet and one of the best known masters in the Bristol and English Channels. The deceased captain was 61 years of age, and was highly respected by a wide circle of friends. A week ago, in conversation with his wife and family, he expressed a wish that he should die at his post, and during the days which followed, made frequent allusions thereto which, in view of the suddenness with which death overtook him, amounted to a premonition. Early on Thursday afternoon he complained of feeling unwell and collapsed, death ensuing a few hours later from a cerebral haemorrhage. The late captain leaves a widow and a large family to mourn his loss.

His was a life of the sea. Gaining his master's certificate at the early age of 18, the sea was followed uninterruptedly up to the time of his death and the seizure took place on one of the Campbell steamers. He had joined the company in 1891 and took command of the *Waverley* in 1894, progressing into the *Cambria* and then to the *Brighton Queen*. The last named was his latest boat, plying between the South Coast resorts and regularly crossing the channel to France....

➤ Capt. West, in his younger days, appears in this photograph taken aboard the *Westward Ho* at Ilfracombe in 1895, seated second from the right. On Capt. West's left is Chief Officer Daniel Taylor (later Captain and Commodore of the White Funnel Fleet). On Capt. West's right is Capt. Peter Campbell and on Capt. Peter's right is Chief Engineer William Docherty. On his right is another engineer, Mr Pocock. Standing behind, with his pipe in his hand and a flower in his buttonhole, is Purser, Mr Peter 'Dandy' Walker. I have been unable to identify the other gentlemen.

➤▼ *Brighton Queen* leaving Boulogne in the 1900s. The trip to Boulogne, with a visit to the Casino, was a great favourite, especially with the more affluent residents of the Brighton district, and it became customary for them to meet regularly on board and to enjoy the sumptuous luncheon and dinner on the journey. Mr Arkell's book continues:

There is no more convenient way to make the acquaintance of our neighbours across the channel than by taking a ticket on Messrs P&A Campbell's fine steamer. As a rule, the earlier portion of the journey is broken by calls at Eastbourne and Hastings, where a further contingent of passengers wait expectantly upon the landing stages. Then the journey begins in earnest. Soon all trace of land is left behind and some passengers, less travelled than their fellows, experience for the first time the novelty of being on the open sea. This stage of the journey is usually devoted to the discussion of an excellent lunch, for the company are their own caterers and spare no pains to give their patrons satisfaction in this important respect.

There is just time to finish coffee and a cigar before the French coast begins to show through the haze. Then all eyes are turned ahead. The dome of the cathedral is the first outstanding landmark to rivet the attention, and less important features of the landscape follow in their turn. Thus, it is soon possible to make out the little village of Wimereux, lying just away to the left, and the Casino which is in a direct line with the entrance to the harbour. The slow passage to the quay is something in the nature of a triumphal progress...

A. C. — 89. BOULOGNE-SUR-MER. — Les Bateaux d'Excursions dans le Port.

◄ Contrasting steamers at Boulogne, 1902/1903. In the centre of the trio is the *Brighton Queen*, on a trip from Brighton, Eastbourne and Hastings. On her starboard side is the Hastings, St Leonards & Eastbourne Steamboat Co.'s *Alexandra,* from Hastings, and at the inside berth, *La Marguerite,* owned by New Palace Steamers Ltd, from Margate.

The *Brighton Queen* was the mainstay of P&A Campbell's pre-1914 south coast services and carried out not only the continental sailings but also the longer coastal cruises, ranging from Swanage to Deal. She was supported by a variety of smaller vessels: *Albion,* and the four illustrated below.

◄ *Bonnie Doon* arriving at Eastbourne, 1907/1910.

➤ *Glen Rosa* leaving Eastbourne, 1903/1910.

▼ *Waverley* arriving at Eastbourne in 1912.

Palace Pier Brighton (Finest Pier in the World)

Ravenswood arriving at Palace Pier, Brighton, 1913/1914.

◀ *Devonia* arriving at Bournemouth in 1925. It was not until 1923 that P&A Campbell Ltd were able to resume their south coast services, with the sailings following much the same tried and tested pattern of the pre-war years. The *Devonia* took the place of the late, lamented *Brighton Queen*, which had been sunk by an enemy mine off the Belgian coast on 6 October 1915 while on Admiralty service. The *Devonia* was supported initially by the *Ravenswood* and the former Yellow Funnel steamer, *Lady Evelyn,* renamed *Brighton Belle.*

▼ Campbell's second *Waverley* replaced the *Ravenswood* at Brighton in 1926. She is seen here leaving Eastbourne in 1927.

▲ *Brighton Belle* at Littlehampton. Before the war Littlehampton was a frequent port of call for the smaller steamers but the first post-war sailing was not made until the *Brighton Belle* visited on Thursday 25 August 1932. She is seen here on that occasion setting out on her return to Brighton.

▲▼ Aboard *Brighton Belle* in the 1930s approaching one of the guardians of the English Channel shipping lanes. The *Royal Sovereign* light vessel was a frequent 'destination' for the popular short sea cruises from Brighton, Eastbourne and Hastings. When the sea conditions allowed it was not unusual for the steamers to approach the light vessel close enough for bundles of magazines and newspapers, supplied by the passengers, to be thrown aboard. Occasionally families and friends of the light vessel's crew would make the trip to 'shout' the latest domestic news to them.

Brighton Queen (ex-*Lady Moyra*) replaced *Devonia* on the south coast from 1933 and is seen arriving at Bournemouth on 1 August of that year.

▲ *Brighton Queen* and *Glen Gower* at Newhaven in May 1937.

➤ *Glen Gower* leaving a south coast pier in 1938.

A final quote from Reginald Arkell's guide book brings this chapter to a fitting end:

The shadows of evening lengthen on the steamer's promenade deck, and the setting sun tinges the waters of the English Channel with gold. The buoyancy of the voyagers has given place to a more restful contemplation of the beauty of the scene. Some are quietly discussing the incidents of the day, while others prefer to let their thoughts wander at random among the memories of happy hours well spent. Gradually the lights on shore spring to life, and familiar objects take definite shape. Once again the moorings are made secure and the gangways are put out. Tired but happy folk bid each other 'Good-night', and go their separate ways. For a few moments the lights of the pier continue to glow steadily, and then they, too, pass into blackness.

Navy Days

Throughout the era of coastal passenger cruising a boost to the companies' takings was provided by the Royal Navy. During the summer seasons the Admiralty despatched its ships, either singly or in squadrons, to visit or to anchor off a variety of ports and resorts. The pleasure steamer operators took every opportunity to run cruises around the warships and, if circumstances allowed, to land passengers on board them for conducted tours. In addition, the Naval Reviews, at which the might of the British navy was displayed for all to see, attracted huge numbers of passengers, not only by day but also by night, when the spectacle of the fully illuminated warships, often with firework displays, were experiences not to be missed.

Coronation  H.M. King

of   George V.

GRAND
Naval Review & Illuminations
At Spithead, on Saturday, June 24th, 1911.

Special Reserved Excursions by the Magnificent Steamers of P. & A. Campbell, Ltd.
(Weather and circumstances permitting)

"Brighton Queen"

Without exception the most Magnificent, Fastest, and Luxuriously appointed Cross Channel Excursion Steamer plying on the South Coast.

Grand Excursion to Review and Illuminations (From BRIGHTON ONLY)
Leaving Brighton Palace Pier 9.15 a.m., West Pier 9.30 a.m

Steamer will proceed to Spithead, passing up and down the several lines of Fleet, then anchoring to witness Review, after which Passengers will be landed for some time at Ryde, then embarking for Cruise Round Fleet and anchoring to witness Illuminations and thence to Brighton.

"Waverley"

This Magnificent Steamer with Promenade Deck 160 ft. in length, Elaborately Fitted Lounge and Dining Saloons, Fore and Aft, is Second only to "Brighton Queen" among the numerous Excursion Steamers plying on the South Coast.

GRAND EXCURSION TO REVIEW
Leaving Hastings Pier 6.20 a.m., Eastbourne Pier 7.20 a.m., Brighton (West Pier) 9 a.m.

Steamer will proceed to Spithead, passing up and down the several lines of Fleet, then anchoring to witness Review, afterwards touching at Ryde Pier to land Passengers desirous of witnessing Illuminations, thence to Brighton (Back about 8 p.m.), Eastbourne about 9.30 p.m. and Hastings 10.30 p.m.

Fares from Brighton—

Per "BRIGHTON QUEEN" to Review and Illuminations, **31/6.**   Coupon holders, **25/-.**

Per "WAVERLEY" to Review (only), **16/6.**   Coupon holders, **12/6.**

Per "BRIGHTON QUEEN" to Review (only), returning from Ryde to Brighton by "WAVERLEY," back about 8 p.m., **25/-.**   Coupon holders, **20/-.**

Fares from Hastings and Eastbourne—

Per "WAVERLEY" to Review (only), **21/-.**   Coupon holders, **16/6.**

Per "WAVERLEY" to Review, joining "BRIGHTON QUEEN" at Ryde for Illuminations, thence to Brighton, changing at Brighton on home journey to "WAVERLEY," **31/6.**   Coupon holders, **25/-.**

SPECIAL NOTICES:—

I.—In order to ensure the comfort of passengers the numbers of each class of ticket will be **so strictly limited** that at no time shall there be more on board than **Two-thirds** of the carrying capacity as certified by the Board of Trade.

II.—Coupons, Advertising and Complimentary Tickets not available.

III.—Holders of Coupon Books desirous of travelling at reduced fares must present their Coupon Books for endorsement when purchasing tickets.

IV.—In the event of weather preventing steamers making the trips all fares will be refunded in full, and in the event of postponement of Review fares will be refunded less 25 per cent.

CATERING.—Breakfasts, Luncheons, Teas, &c., as well as other refreshments (of the best quality only) will be served in the spacious Saloons and Lounges in the Company's well-known First-Class Style, and at the **usual** low tariff.

TICKETS which must be purchased before 6 p.m. on MONDAY, JUNE 19th, can be obtained from Messrs. THOS. COOK & SON, 81 King's Road, Brighton (Tel. 363 Nat.); or at the various offices of the Company: **Hastings**—P. & A. Campbell, Ltd., Pier (Nat. Tel. 566); **Eastbourne**—Mr. David Smith, 21 Terminus Road, or P. & A. Campbell, Ltd., Pier (Nat. Tel. 117y); **Worthing**—Mr. A. W. Hoare, "Gordon House" (opposite Railway Station); **BRIGHTON**—P. & A. Campbell, Ltd., 70 Ship Street (Nat. Tel. 5991).

Timetable for the Coronation Naval Review of 24 June 1911.

P. & A. CAMPBELL LTD.

SPITHEAD.

THE GREAT ASSEMBLY OF

250 WAR VESSELS.

MAGNIFICENT ILLUMINATIONS AND SEARCHLIGHT DISPLAY

IN THE EVENING.

SPECIAL AFTERNOON & EVENING EXCURSIONS

BY THE CROSS CHANNEL STEAMERS,

DEVONIA & BRIGHTON BELLE

Well equipped with fine Saloons, and Catering a speciality.

SATURDAY, JULY 26th

The "BRIGHTON BELLE" leaves Brighton Palace Pier 2.45 p.m., West Pier 3 p.m. for a Cruise through the various lines of Warships, afterwards takes up her position to witness the Illuminations, then returning to Brighton. Back about 2 a.m.

Tickets obtained before the day, **8/6**; on the day, **10/6.**

From Messrs. THOS. COOK & SON, 81, King's Road, Brighton, or at the Company's Office, 7, Old Steine, Brighton.

SATURDAY, JULY 26th

Evening Trip to Spithead to View the Illuminations.

The "DEVONIA" leaves Brighton Palace Pier 6.50 p.m., West Pier 7 p.m. and takes up her position in time to see the Marvellous Exhibition of 250 War Vessels Illuminated, then returning to Brighton. Back about 1.30 a.m. Fare 5/-

Full particulars may be obtained from P. & A. CAMPBELL Ltd., 7, Old Steine, Brighton. W. REID, Agent.

The Southern Publishing Co., Ltd., 130, North Street, Brighton. P8404.

Timetable for the Naval Review of 1924.

With Ryde, Isle of Wight, in the background, the *Brighton Belle* arrives alongside an unidentified warship at anchor in Spithead on Sunday 27 July 1924. This was an unusual destination for the diminutive steamer, the normal extent of her sailings at that time being Brighton, Eastbourne and Hastings.

Devonia leaving Eastbourne in July 1929. She is taking passengers to board the warship HMS *Nelson*, which is partially visible astern of her.

◄ Passengers crowd the deck of the *Brighton Belle* on their way to visit the cruiser HMS *Frobisher,* at anchor off Hastings, on Monday 30 July 1934. For this occasion she was issued with a special certificate allowing her to carry 1,023 passengers – nearly 300 more than her usual maximum.

➤ Aboard the *Brighton Belle,* alongside HMS *Frobisher,* Monday 30 July 1934. HMS *Frobisher* was one of a class of five cruisers built to a First World War design in the early 1920s. She and one of her consorts, HMS *Hawkins,* also saw a good deal of action in the Second World War until 1944 when they both became accommodation ships prior to being laid up before scrapping.

Some of the *Frobisher*'s crew pay a reciprocal visit to the *Brighton Belle*. They must have found the difference between the two ships staggering!

Bristol Queen and *Cardiff Queen* anchored in Spithead for the Coronation Naval Review on Monday 15 June 1953. At the Review the White Funnel Fleet was represented by three steamers: *Cardiff Queen* (which spent the whole of the season on the Sussex coast, as she had done in 1952), together with the *Glen Gower* and the *Bristol Queen* from the Bristol Channel. All three vessels ran a variety of cruises around the assembled fleet during the week before the review.

Bristol Queen leaving Bournemouth Pier, 11 June 1953.

Bristol Queen at the Royal Naval Review, Monday 15 June 1953. She was temporarily fitted with radar for her visit as well as a canvas awning over her after deckhouse which was intended to shield passengers from the sun. In fact, it sheltered them from the rain! Review Day was very wet.

Wartime

In common with many other excursion vessels, the steamers of P&A Campbell Ltd were requisitioned by the Admiralty in both world wars to act principally as minesweepers. The arduous duties which they and their personnel were called upon to perform could hardly have been in greater contrast to those for which they were intended, and some did not return. Yet their work was vital and of inestimable value to the war effort.

The history of the White Funnel steamers' involvement in the two world wars is described in detail in my two books, *A Dangerous Occupation* and *On Admiralty Service*. However, further research has brought some very interesting facts to light.

Chief Officer James Martin at the wheel of the *Ravenswood* in 1947. Mr Martin was one of the 'old school' of P&A Campbell officers who, until his retirement in 1951, still wore a wing collar, always donned his kid gloves before handling any item of bridge brass work, and was rarely seen without a white handkerchief in his top pocket.

This photograph, and the two illustrations which follow it, are reproduced by courtesy of Mr Martin's grand daughter, Mrs Elaine Bealing, to whom I wish to express my sincere thanks for permission to publish the illustrations and for the biographical details of her grandfather. I also wish to express my gratitude to my good friend Mr Ken Jenkins for much practical help, including supplying the copies, and for bringing my attention to the wartime incident outlined below.

James Martin was born in Wellington, Somerset, in 1879 and joined P&A Campbell Ltd in 1897 as a deckhand. It appears that he worked on the White Funnel steamers during the summer seasons and went 'deep sea' during the winter months. He left the Campbells at the end of 1904 and, in the following year, joined the Barry Railway Steamers, working his way up through the ranks with them and their subsequent owners, Bristol Channel Passenger Boats Ltd., until their remaining steamers became part of the White Funnel Fleet in 1912. He had passed the examination of competency as 'Mate' at Newport on 12 December 1907. He never progressed to the rank of master but this was from personal choice and not lack of ability. Mr George Owen knew him well and described him not only as a great character

but also a 'prime seaman, much respected by all his fellow officers'.

When war was declared in August 1914 he was Chief Officer of the *Devonia*. She and the *Brighton Queen* were chosen to undertake minesweeping trials in the Bristol Channel. They proved eminently suitable for the task and their commissioning into the Royal Navy pioneered the requisitioning of many more of the country's pleasure steamers.

Mr Martin served aboard the *Devonia* throughout the war. She was the flagship of a fleet of eight sweepers, known as the 'Devonia Unit', which operated in the North Sea, initially from Grimsby but later on the Tyne. Generally the minesweepers worked in pairs but the commander of the Devonia Unit, Lieutenant Commander W.V. Rice, together with his highly trained personnel, habitually swept with no fewer than five sweepers abreast, towing four sweep wires between them.

On one such operation several enemy mines became entangled in the sweep and were hauled to the surface hard under the *Devonia*'s stern. This lethal situation was brought to a satisfactory conclusion thanks to the bravery of Chief Petty Officer Martin who climbed over the stern armed with a hammer and cold chisel and proceeded to part the sweep wire. The relief at the sight of the mines drifting away, followed by their destruction by gunfire can only be imagined!

For this extraordinary act of courage CPO Martin was awarded the Distinguished Service Medal, presented to him by His Majesty King George V at an award ceremony at Immingham on 10 April 1918.

VISIT OF THEIR MAJESTIES THE KING AND QUEEN,
Wednesday, 10th April, 1918.

No. W.1924.
MEMORANDUM.

With reference to paragraph 6 of my Memorandum No. W.1924 of 2nd April, 1918, the following Officers and men who will be decorated by His Majesty are to fall in in the order given :—

Name, etc.	Ship.	Decoration.
Captain Berwick Curtis, D.S.O., R.N.	Abdiel	Bar to D.S.O.
„ F. E. Massey-Dawson „	Pekin	D.S.O.
Comdr. Wyndham-Forbes, ret. „	Wallington	„
Act.-Sqn.-Cdr. Fred. G. Hards, R.N.A.S.	Killingholme	D.S.C.
Lieut. R. N. Oliver, R.N.	Telemachus	„
Flight-Lieut. H. M. Morris, R.N.A.S.	Killingholme	„
Flight-Lieut. J. R. Crouch „	Howden	„
Lieut. D. Jefferson, R.N.R.	Wallington for Lordship ...	„
„ J. Pollok, „	„ Arctic Whale	„
x „ R. M. Jackson, ... „	Satellite for Lord Reading	„
x „ J. M. James, ... „	Island Prince	„
x Engr.-Lieut. J. Black, „	„	„
Lieut. J. A. Campbell, act. ... „	Wallington for Wm. Tennant	„
„ W. L. Cook, „	Pekin	„
„ H. Klugh, R.N.V.R.	„	„
Mr. A. G. Stock, Gunner R.N.	Abdiel	„
„ J. Watson, late Skipper ... R.N.R.	Wallington for Oldham ...	„
„ J. S. Macey, „ „	Thalia	„
C.P.O. C. H. Grant	Pekin	D.S.M.
x Chief Motor Mech. J. Primrose	Satellite for M.L. 7 ...	„
„ E.R.A. T. Hewitt	Crane	„
x 2nd Hand C. J. Webster, ... R.N.R.	Kingfisher	„
„ H. V. Wright, ... „	Wallington for Prefect ...	„
x C.P.O. J. Martin ... M.F.A.	Island Prince for Devonia ...	„
2nd Hand H. Mayes, R.N.R.	Pekin for St. Leonard ...	„
„ M. Wisher „	„ Brackonlynn ...	„
Petty Officer G. A. Jeune ... „	Wallington for Helvetia ...	„
„ „ F. F. Lynch ... „	Pekin	Bar to D.S.M.
„ „ A. V. Bodiam ... R.F.R.	Doon	D.S.M.
Sto. P.O. E. J. Symonds „	Boyne	„
Sto. P.O. E. H. Tennant „	Greyhound	„
Yeo. Sig. J. H. McArdle „	Garry	„
„ C. R. Robins „	Legion	„
x Ldg. Deck Hand G. Colman ... R.N.R.	Halcyon	„
„ „ F. W. Brown „	Pekin for Royal Irvin ...	„
Sig. L. Evans ... R.N.V.R.	Wallington for Lordship ...	„
x Engineman T. R. Clementson, R.N.R.T.	Island Prince	„
x „ R. Boak, ... R.N.R.	„ for Recepto ...	„
„ J. P. Thompson ... „	Wallington for Wm. Tennant	„
x Able Seaman B. E. Lewis ... „	P 57	„
x Able Seaman J. T. Poulter „	P 57	„
Deckhand A. R. Thompson ... R.N.R.	Wallington for White Rose II	„
x „ T. Morrison ... „	Satellite for Dollar Princess	„
x „ A. Aitchison ... „	Satellite for Beatrice ...	„
x „ W. B. Darnall ... „	Island Prince	„
Trimmer S. Balls ... „	Pekin for Waldorf ...	„
Widow of T. D. Bass, Deckhand „	Corientes	„

2. Separate copies of this Memorandum are being supplied for each Officer and man concerned.

3. Arrangements have been made for those marked " x " to report to Commanding Officer, R.N. Depot, Immingham, on 9th April.

4. Officers are to be responsible for the attendance of Officers and men under their orders as follows :—

Flag Captain for those attached to Auxiliary Patrol Vessels in Area IX.
Commanding Officer, R.N. Depot, for those marked x and Mrs. Bass.
P.M.S.O. for those from Pekin.
C.D. 20 for vessels of 20th Destroyer Flotilla.
C.D. 7 for vessels of 7th Destroyer Flotilla.

5. As soon as His Majesty has finished inspecting the ranks, all those mentioned in paragraph 1, will be ordered to fall out and will proceed without delay to the position ordered to the south of the dais, and they will fall in in the order given—Officers in the front rank, C.P.O.'s, P.O.'s and men in the rear rank facing towards the dais.

After receiving their decoration each Officer or man should fall in on the opposite side of the dais, until the parade is dismissed.

6. Mrs. Bass, with her daughter, has been directed to come to Immingham by the electric tram due at 9.50 a.m. Commander Anderson is to arrange for her to be met and conducted to the Parade Ground.

The Memorandum listing the recipients of awards. CPO Martin's name can be found under the heading of his 'ship' Island Prince – the shore establishment under which the *Devonia* and her consorts served. (Ken Jenkins Collection)

VIRTUTE ET INDUSTRIA

The Lord Mayor, Sheriff, and Citizens of Bristol desire to tender their hearty congratulations and to express their high appreciation of the gallant heroism which so nobly won the great honour which has been conferred upon you.

.... Lord Mayor

.... Sheriff

ROYAL MERCANTILE MARINE RESERVE.   Chf. P. Ofr. James Martin.   D.S.M.

After the war the City of Bristol acknowledged Mr Martin's gallant action by the certificate reproduced here and also by requesting him to lead the marine contingent in the peace procession through the city to the Colston Hall. (Ken Jenkins Collection)

At the award ceremony at Immingham another P&A Campbell employee was honoured. This was Chief Engineer John Black of the *Westward Ho*. 'Johnny' Black, as he was known, was a long-serving engineer with the company both before and after the war and had escaped potentially fatal injury earlier during the conflict in an incident mentioned in a report to the First Sea Lord:

Near the Swarte Bank a mine exploded under the *Westward Ho*'s stern, taking the kite, still attached to its wire, into the air. It described a semi-circle and came down between the paddle boxes. Although it broke through the deck and into the engine room it did not damage the machinery nor the Chief Engineer who was on the platform at the time.

John Black was awarded the Distinguished Service Cross for keeping his ship at sea for longer, in the course of a year, than any other paddler.

➤ John Black appears in this photograph taken aboard the *Brighton Queen* at Ilfracombe on Thursday 21 June 1934, on her way from Bristol to Brighton. He is the moustached gentleman seated on the left of the front row. Next to him is Capt. Bill Couves and on Capt. Couves' left is Chief Officer, (later Captain) H. Fuller. In the back row, from left to right: 2nd engineer, (name unknown); Syd Partington, Purser; Tom Smith, Purser/Radio Officer; W. Bilson, Chief Steward and 3rd engineer (name unknown).

Second World War

➤ HMS *Glen Gower* at her berth at the Fish Quay, North Shields, in 1941. The *Glen Gower,* along with most of her consorts, was requisitioned by the Admiralty shortly after the outbreak of war in 1939, initially as a minesweeper and later as an anti-aircraft ship. This story, however, begins when she was a member of the 8th Minesweeping Flotilla, based on the River Tyne, and concerns the Dutch cargo vessel *Ottoland.*

The *Ottoland*'s voyage had brought her across the North Atlantic Ocean from the Canadian port of Buctouche, with a cargo of pit props bound for Immingham. Having reached Methil, on the Firth of Forth, she joined a convoy which set off on the journey south to the Humber, but struck a stray magnetic acoustic mine about fifteen miles east of Sunderland on Saturday 5 October 1940. The *Glen Gower,* part of the minesweeping force accompanying the convoy through its section of the War Channel, was first at the scene. She steamed through a seemingly endless amount of timber, which had been washed from the *Ottoland*'s deck as she sank, before reaching the ship's lifeboats and rescuing all forty-three members of her crew. (Eric Rees)

➤ The *Ottoland* sinking. (PSPS Archives)

▲ A last glimpse of the *Ottoland*. Her crew were disembarked at North Shields later in the day, and after expressing their eternal gratitude to Lt. Commander M. A. Biddulph and his ship's company, went on their way. Similarly, the officers and crew of the *Glen Gower* resumed their minesweeping duties almost as though nothing had happened; they were simply getting on with the job. (Eric Rees)

▼ ➤ But fifteen years later the incident came to light in a most surprising manner, when a letter and photograph were received at P&A Campbell's office in Bristol. I wish to thank my good friend, Mr Andrew Gladwell, Curator of the Paddle Steamer Preservation Society Archives, for bringing the matter to my attention. The letter and photograph speak for themselves.

▲ Survivors of the *Ottoland* climbing aboard *Glen Gower*. (Eric Rees)

Your Ref. JWJ/GEL.

R'dam 1-10-'55

Messrs P. & A. Campbell Ltd
1 Britannia Buildings
Cumberland Basin
Bristol 8.

Dear Sirs,

Many thanks for your kind letter of the 8th July '55 with 2 photographs of your S/s. "Glen Gower". I am very much obliged for these. There is a story attached to this. Enclosed please find two photographs where your ship was involved in 1940.

I was master mariner on board the Dutch steamer "OTTOLAND" when she was blown up by magnetic-acoustic mine on Oct the 5th 1940. All hands were saved by the British minesweeper "Glen Gower" and landed at North-Shields East Coast U.K. on Oct the 5th 1940. 15 years ago. I don't know if there are any of your crew still in service on board today. Please put these photo's up in the saloon to commemorate an act of humanity if you desire to do so. If you are interested in the full story of the act I will be pleased

2

pleased to let you know same.
It was thro' an article in the
Shipbuilding 12-5-55 that my
attention was drawn to your ship.
Via the Shipbuilding Record office
your address was passed on to me.
Believe me Gentlemen that I
sign with many kind feelings to
the owners of the "Glen Gower"
Yours faithfully
H. Tichelaar

H. TIGCHELAAR
Ex. MASTER DUTCH
s/s. "OTTOLAND"

18ᴮ HUYGENSSTR
ROTTERDAM (W).

P.S. Behind the duffel coated Capt R.N.,
with white collar, that's me.
HARRY.

The Pre-war Paddle Steamers – Post-war

After the Second World War only four paddle steamers remained to resume the company's services. They were *Ravenswood, Glen Usk, Glen Gower* and *Britannia,* all of which were in need of extensive refits to prepare them for passenger carrying once again.

They returned to Bristol at intervals during 1945 and, despite severe shortages of materials and manpower, all except the *Glen Gower* recommenced sailing in 1946, although on a very limited timetable for that season. It was not until 1948 that the White Funnel Fleet reached its full post-war strength.

▲▼ *Ravenswood* undergoing her post-war refit at the Underfall Yard early in 1946. In appearance she suffered from the contemporary trend for concealed paddle boxes. Gone were the graceful arched curves and fanned louvres radiating from the central, semicircular emblem, as had her varnished wood bridge, replaced with a strictly utilitarian box-like metal structure. However, such details were unimportant to the passengers who boarded her for the first post-war trip – a cruise from Bristol to off Clevedon – on the afternoon of Saturday 13 April 1946. They were only too delighted to enjoy the sea air again and to know that the White Funnel Fleet was back in business! (PSPS archives)

▲ Edwin Keen's magnificent photograph of *Britannia* passing Battery Point, Portishead, on her way from Bristol to Clevedon, Cardiff, Penarth, Barry and Ilfracombe on Saturday 22 June 1946.

◄ *Britannia* at Ilfracombe. June/July 1946. This photograph is reproduced by courtesy of Mr Peter Southcombe, a former traffic manager of P&A Campbell Ltd, who states:

It was taken, by the look of it, on a flood tide and I guess that the party near the bow had been tightening the bow ropes; it looks as though they had already done the springs. They appear to be doing something to the rigging of the foremast as well, with Capt. Brander looking on. Interestingly, you can see on the extreme left of the photograph, in the field above the rocks, a part of one of the two gun emplacements which were built above Raparee cove and which contained very ancient weapons, said to be more dangerous to the gunners than to any enemy! The gunners were elderly reservists and I only heard of them firing a practice shot once, when they were installed in 1940. Both emplacements were demolished in about 1950.

Britannia was in service until the early hours of Saturday 20 July when part of her 'haystack' boiler collapsed while lying at the Pier Head, Cardiff. All her subsequent sailings were cancelled and she was towed to Bristol to lay up. She would not sail again until 1948.

▲ At the time of the withdrawal of the *Britannia,* the refit of the *Glen Usk,* at Charles Hill & Sons yard, was nearing completion. Hill's and P&A Campbell's workforce then worked around the clock to bring her into service as quickly as possible. They achieved the remarkable feat of completing the job in less than a week! The *Glen Usk* is seen here in the Cumberland Basin on Wednesday 24 July 1946, the day on which she entered service. (Edwin Keen)

➤ *Glen Gower* nearing completion of her post-war refit at Bristol, Sunday 6 March 1947. She had experienced just over five years of very arduous war service and returned to Bristol in a very bad condition on 25 June 1945. Her refit included the building of a new bridge and a completely new promenade deck, as well as major alterations to her accommodation. The work was completed in time for her to reopen the company's south coast sailings when she resumed calls from Brighton on Wednesday 21 May 1947. (Ernest Nurse)

◄ The *Britannia*'s 'haystack' boiler could be neither repaired nor replaced; that type of boiler was already outdated when it was installed in 1935. Negotiations took place between P&A Campbell Ltd and the Admiralty who agreed that the boiler's collapse was exacerbated by repeated shocks from the exploding of mines in her sweeps during the early part of the war, as well as hard steaming with little time allowed for maintenance.

They agreed to pay £24,000 towards the cost of a replacement – this is believed to have been 95 per cent of the total cost. A large, double-ended boiler was installed, which necessitated two funnels and a variety of other alterations, including the removal of her after deckhouse and two forward lifeboats. She is seen here at Charles Hill's yard in April 1948 having just received a coat of anti-rust paint. (Cyril Hawkins Garrington)

▼ After the completion of her painting, and having run satisfactory boiler trials, *Britannia* was stationed on the south coast for the 1948 and 1949 seasons. She is seen here making an evening arrival at Brighton. (PSPS Archives)

▲ *Glen Gower* leaving Swansea in 1948. (H.G. Owen)

◄ *Glen Gower* backing out of Ilfracombe into the Bristol Channel swell in 1948. (H.G. Owen)

Glen Gower at anchor off Lundy, Tuesday 23 August 1949. (Edwin Keen)

Glen Gower at the Porthcawl breakwater in the early 1950s. (Gordon Thomas)

▲ *Britannia* arriving at Ilfracombe from Lundy, on her return to Barry, Penarth and Cardiff, Thursday 22 June 1950. (H.G. Owen)

◄ Ilfracombe in the summer of 1950. *Britannia,* from Cardiff and Barry, is leaving for Lundy while the *Cardiff Queen,* from Swansea, lies at anchor in The Range. (PSPS Archives)

➤ *Britannia* at Minehead 1951/1953.

▼ *Ravenswood* arriving at Minehead in 1951. In the foreground is the ketch, *Emma Louise*, once a frequent visitor to the Bristol Channel and often seen in Minehead harbour.

THE HARBOUR, MINEHEAD

Ravenswood and *Britannia* in the Merchant's dock, Bristol, in May 1952. The *Ravenswood* has already been dry-docked and her external painting is under way in readiness to begin her season at Whitsun. The *Britannia,* as yet untouched externally, was not due to start her season until early July. (Donald Anderson)

Britannia in the Avon on Saturday 2 August 1952. This was a particularly arduous day for the 'Brit' and her personnel. She left Cardiff at 07.00 for Penarth, Barry and Ilfracombe from where she ran a day trip, departing at 10.15, to Lynmouth, Barry, Penarth, Cardiff, Clevedon and Bristol with a cruise in the River Severn to off the mouth of the River Wye.

The photograph shows her returning to Bristol from the cruise in time to take her 17.15 return from Bristol to Clevedon, Cardiff, Penarth, Barry, Lynmouth and Ilfracombe. Her final trip of the day took her from Ilfracombe, at 22.15, to Barry, Penarth and Cardiff where she arrived just before 02.00 on Sunday – nearly a nineteen-hour day! (Edwin Keen)

◄ *Glen Usk* arriving at Ilfracombe in 1952.

▼ *Ravenswood* arriving at Weston on Wednesday 16 June 1954.
(Norman Bird)

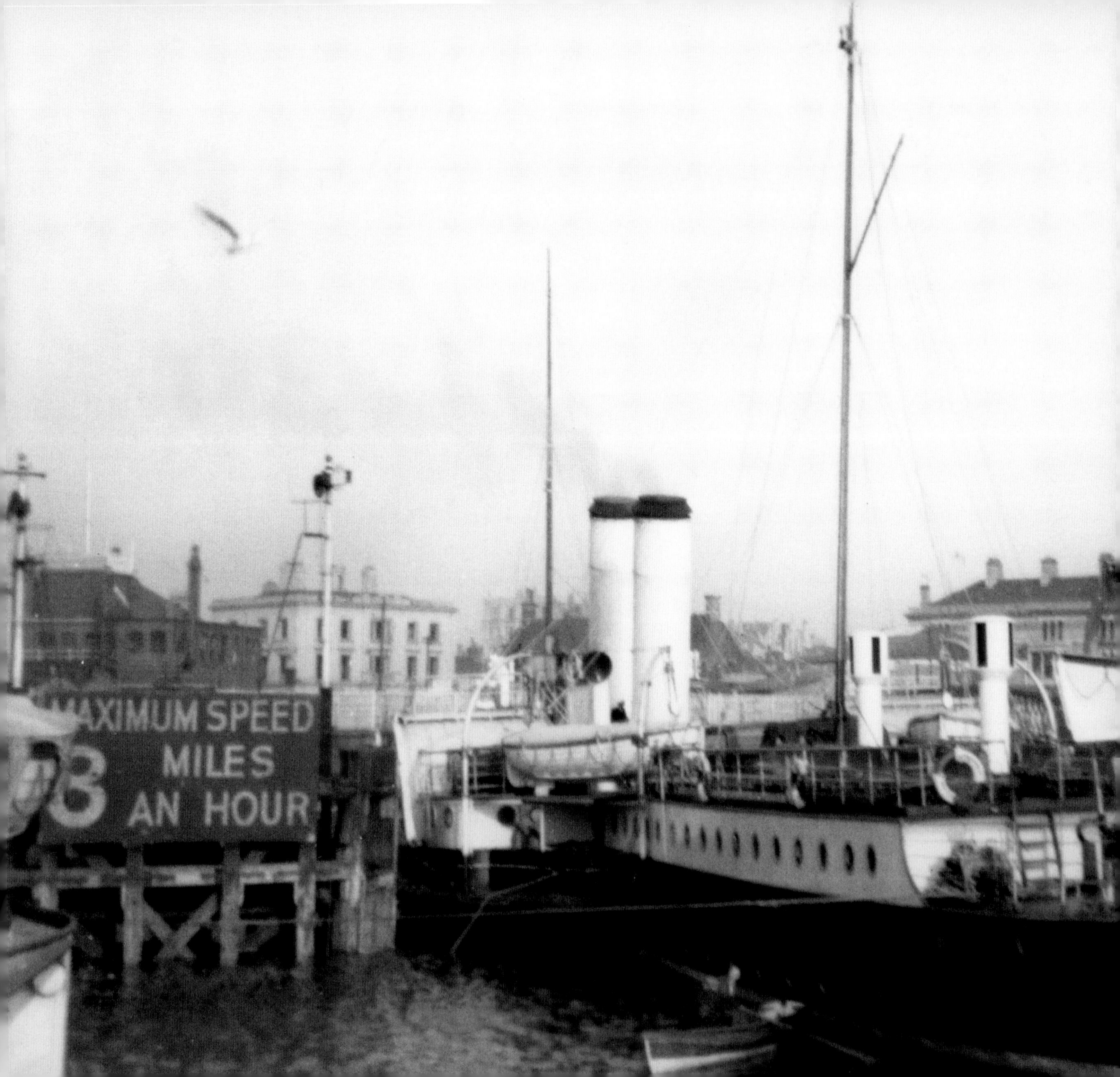
MAXIMUM SPEED
3 MILES
AN HOUR

◄ *Britannia* at the Pier Head, Cardiff, on Monday 24 September 1956, two days before her final withdrawal from service. (John Brown)

As the 1950s progressed and one bad summer followed another, P&A Campbell Ltd found itself in serious financial difficulties. Furthermore, the four ageing post-war paddle steamers were in need of increasingly more extensive and expensive repairs and refurbishment, but the company simply did not have the money. Although they 'hung on' by a very slender financial thread, economic pressures ultimately enforced their withdrawal from service and they all ended their days in the breakers' yard.

▼ *Ravenswood* passing Avonmouth in tow for Cashmore's yard at Newport, 20 October 1955. (Edwin Keen)

➤ *Britannia* at Cashmore's yard, Newport, in December 1956. (H.G. Owen)

▼ The sadly dilapidated *Glen Gower* in the Penarth dock basin on 7 April 1960. Alongside her is the United Towing Co.'s tug, *Tradesman,* which towed her to the breakers' yard in Antwerp.

➤ *Glen Usk* in the Queen Alexandra dock, Cardiff, with the tug, *Talbot*, which towed her to the breaker's yard, Monday 29 April 1963. (Chris Collard)

▼ A view of Haulbowline Industries' yard at Passage West, Cork, in May 1963 with the demolition of the *Glen Usk* well under way.

The final vestiges of the last of the pre-war
White Funnel steamers.

The Post-war 'Queens'

The last two paddle steamers to be built for P&A Campbell Ltd, to replace, in some measure, their war losses, were the *Bristol Queen* and *Cardiff Queen,* both of which were destined to lead tragically short lives of just over twenty years. It is a fitting tribute to that long line of white-funnelled vessels to end this volume with a series of photographs of the much loved, post-war Queens.

➤▼ (*and opposite*) The first of the post-war White Funnel paddle steamers. This view, taken on 22 December 1945, and the following three photographs, taken on 1 January 1946, all by Graham E. Langmuir, show No.334 under construction at the Albion dockyard of Charles Hill & Sons, Bristol. (PSPS Archives)

The launch of No.334 on Thursday 4 April 1946. The local press reported:

More than 3,000 people saw the *Bristol Queen* launched this afternoon from the Albion Dockyard. A moment before Bert Sage pulled the launching
lever, a bottle of Bristol Milk – the city's famous sherry – was released by the Lady Mayoress (Mrs James Owen) to smack against the ship's bow.
It did not break, and an official dashed forward and grabbed the red, white and blue ribbon hanging from the bottle and handed it back to the Lady
Mayoress, who was just in time to send the bottle crashing back, this time to break as the vessel glided away amid a tremendous cheer.

◄▼ *Above and below*: The engines of the *Bristol Queen* nearing completion at Rankin & Blackmore's engineering works, Greenock, on 20 May 1946. They were transported by road to Bristol for installation at Charles Hill's yard. (Graham E. Langmuir)

▲ *Bristol Queen* leaving Bristol for trials on Saturday 7 September 1946. As a precaution she was under tow of the tug *John King* to assist her in manoeuvring in the river if the necessity arose.

◄ On the bridge of the *Bristol Queen* at Avonmouth shortly before leaving for further trials on Sunday 8 September 1946. The party consists of directors and guests of P&A Campbell Ltd, as well as representatives of her builders. The only people I can positively identify are the gentleman in uniform, Capt. J.A. Harris, her master for her short 1946 season, and on his right Campbell's managing director, Mr William J. Banks.

▲ *Bristol Queen* entered service on Saturday 14 September 1946 and is seen leaving Cardiff later that month, on her way from Bristol to Ilfracombe.

➤ *Bristol Queen* off Clevedon in 1946. (PSPS Archives)

▲ The second post-war paddle steamer just before her launch at Fairfield yard, Govan, Glasgow, on Wednesday 26 February 1947. The ceremony was performed by Mrs Banks, the wife of Campbell's managing director, who named the ship *Cardiff Queen*. (Graham E. Langmuir)

▲ *Cardiff Queen* off Gourock on Monday 16 June 1947. This was the day on which she left Glasgow for Bristol but her departure was delayed in the Firth of Clyde owing to engine trouble. This photograph was taken during the evening while her engineers were carrying out repairs. She eventually left Gourock at 22.30 that night. (Graham E. Langmuir)

▼ Towards the end of her first season, spent mostly on the Cardiff to Ilfracombe service, the rather unkempt *Cardiff Queen* arrives at Swansea from Ilfracombe on Saturday 9 September 1947. (H.G. Owen)

▲ *Bristol Queen* at anchor in The Range, off Ilfracombe in 1947. (PSPS Archives)

◄ *Bristol Queen* leaving Ilfracombe for a cruise to Bideford Bay in 1947. Astern of her, in the distance, the *Glen Gower* approaches on her way from Swansea. (H.G. Owen)

▲ *Cardiff Queen* arriving at Ilfracombe after lying at anchor offshore, August 1949. (H.G. Owen)

◄ A heavy swell follows the *Cardiff Queen* on her port quarter as she makes her way from Ilfracombe to Swansea on the evening of Saturday 26 August 1950. (H.G. Owen)

▲➤ *Cardiff Queen* at Ilfracombe in 1951.

She had been moored at the inner berth, between the stone bench and the wall of the inner harbour. It was not unusual for this berth to be used during the pre-war years when the company had a larger fleet, but in the post-war years it was not a common occurrence.

However, during the summer of 1951 the stone bench was under reconstruction as part of the major renovation of the whole pier and could not be used. Most of the steamers used the inner berth from time to time in that season, provided the tide served, but these are the only photographs yet to have appeared showing a steamer turning to make her departure. (PSPS Archives)

◄ Until the mid-1950s the *Bristol Queen* rarely visited Swansea, if at all. She was, however, photographed leaving there on Thursday 24 June 1954 on what is believed to have been her first visit to the South Wales port. She was deputising on that and the following two days for the *Cardiff Queen* (the Swansea-based steamer from 1954 to 1958) which was undergoing paddle wheel repairs at Cardiff. The *Bristol Queen* is shown leaving the berth at Pockett's Wharf on the River Tawe.

▼ *Bristol Queen* leaving Swansea in 1955. Having passed through the east and west breakwaters at the mouth of the river, speed is increased to half until she reaches the Swansea Fairway Buoy when 'full ahead' will be maintained to take her across the channel to Ilfracombe. Post-war calls at Mumbles were not resumed until the rebuilding of the pier was completed in 1956.

➤ The rural surroundings of the River Torridge make a pleasing backdrop to Norman Bird's delightful photograph of the *Cardiff Queen* leaving Bideford on Saturday 2 July 1955.

▼ *Cardiff Queen* in the River Usk on Sunday 31 July 1955. The two Queens were infrequent visitors to Newport and when they did call their sailings were usually advertised as 'Specials'. One such trip was made by the *Cardiff Queen* on Sunday 31 July 1955 and was packed to capacity. It was an afternoon cruise to Bristol – always a very popular trip.

On the following day the *South Wales Argus* reported that crowds of potential passengers had been queuing for over three hours when the *Cardiff Queen* arrived at the landing stage from Avonmouth. Mr S.C. Smith Cox, Campbell's managing director, told the reporter that it was the biggest crowd seen at Newport for 25 years, and estimated there must have been about 2,500 people waiting. He added that only 200 had booked but that they would take as many as possible. In fact, that afternoon the *Cardiff Queen* carried her maximum number of 1,107 passengers. (W.T. Collard)

➤ *Bristol Queen* at Tenby c.1956/1958. (John Brown Collection)

▼ *Cardiff Queen* astern of the *Bristol Queen* nine miles north-west of Ilfracombe. On the afternoon of Sunday 19 August 1956 the *Bristol Queen* left Ilfracombe at 13.42 bound for Tenby. At 14.25 she came to a sudden halt owing to serious paddle trouble which completely disabled her. A radio message for assistance was sent to the *Cardiff Queen,* which had left Ilfracombe at 14.15 for Porthcawl and Mumbles.

On her arrival at the scene at about 15.00, when this photograph was taken, the *Bristol Queen* was rolling in the swell, but after skilful manoeuvring by Capt. George Gunn his crew succeeded in reaching the *Bristol Queen* with a tow rope. The towing operation began at 15.35 and the two ships arrived in Swansea Bay four hours later when the *Bristol Queen* was taken into the Prince of Wales Dock by two tugs. On the following day she was towed to Bristol for repairs and was back in service on 25 August.

PLEASURE STEAMER AND CASTLE HILL, TENBY   W 6545

Cardiff Queen approaching Barry harbour on Tuesday 24 April, her first day in service in 1962. (Chris Collard)

◄ *Cardiff Queen* arriving at Pier Head, Cardiff, on 19 May 1965. (Chris Collard)

▼ *Bristol Queen* arriving at Weston in 1963. (Chris Collard)

Bristol Queen leaving Padstow on 28 July 1966. (Norman Bird)

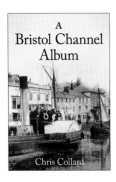

A Bristol Channel Album

CHRIS COLLARD

Chris Collard takes us on a trip down the Bristol Channel, looking at the varied shipping found in the bottom reaches of the Severn. From P&A Campbell paddle steamers to the shipping going in and out of Bristol and Avonmouth Docks, all aspects of Bristol Channel shipping are covered from the 1950s, 1960s and 1970s. Beautifully depicted in rare photographs are P&A Campbell paddle steamers, packet steamers – the forerunners of the excursion steamers, as well as the other companies who took up the challenge of Bristol Channel pleasure cruising. The author has also taken the opportunity to incorporate a certain amount of 'White Funnel Trivia' – some details of a more domestic nature but which, nevertheless, form an integral part of P&A Campbell operations. Shipping enthusiasts and the general reader alike are sure to find this book an interesting account of one of Britain's most famous stretches of water.

978 0 7524 4415 4

A White Funnel Album

CHRIS COLLARD

The White Funnel Fleet of P&A Campbell was an icon of the paddle steamers' heyday, whose vessels were famous from the Bristol Channel to Brighton, a memorable sight for hundreds of thousands who lived in the Bristol Channel area, Brighton and the south coast and Southampton. *A White Funnel Album* is a record in images of one of the most celebrated paddle steamer lines. Using stunning professional photographs and atmospheric holidaymakers' snaps, largely compiled from previously unpublished collections, this volume traces the history of the Fleet from the turn of the century, via the paddlers' wartime service and the glittering inter-war years, to the end of their era in the 1950s. It also includes some of the quirkier and more domestic details of the glory days of paddling, as well as covering famous steamers, their glamorous destinations and the personalities who made the Fleet what it was.

978 0 7524 4698 1

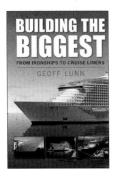

Building the Biggest
FROM IRONSHIPS TO CRUISE LINERS

GEOFF LUNN

In 1843 Brunel's ironship *Great Britain* was launched, becoming the forerunner of the great steel-hulled ships of today. Yet she was tiny compared with the transatlantic liners of the early 1900s as ship-owners vied for the top spot in terms of speed, elegance and size. If the innovative engineers of the Victorian age guided the shipping industry from sail to steam, wood to iron and later to steel, then the twentieth-century invention of the computer took ship construction to entirely new concepts. Today Royal Caribbean's sister ships *Oasis of the Seas* and *Allure of the Seas* are the first passenger ships in history to exceed 200,000 gros tons, measuring seventy times the size of the first Victorian passenger-carrying ironship.

978 0 7524 5079 7

Brunel in South Wales
VOLUME III: LINKS WITH LEVIATHANS

STEPHEN K. JONES

This illustrated history focuses on Brunel's contribution to the maritime world, from his work on dry docks and shipping facilities to his steamships, including his 'great leviathan'. For PSS *Great Eastern*, Brunel chose Milford Haven as a home port where she would spend many years, still the largest ship in the world but sadly without work after her pioneering role laying telegraph cables under the world's oceans. One of Brunel's last engineering projects was a steam railway ferry across the Severn, a unique work that was superseded with the opening of the Severn Tunnel. This illustrated history delves deep into Brunel's legacy.

978 0 7524 4912 8

Visit our website and discover thousands of other History Press books. **www.thehistorypress.co.uk**

The History Press